W9-BZB-462

Cats, Cats, Cats

Short-Haired Cat Breeds

by Christina Mia Gardeski

CAPSTONE PRESS
a capstone imprint

Pebble Plus is published by Capstone Press,
1710 Roe Crest Drive, North Mankato, Minnesota 56003
www.mycapstone.com

Library of Congress Cataloging-in-Publication Data
Cataloging-in-publication information is on file with the Library of Congress.
ISBN 978-1-5157-0958-9 (library binding)
ISBN 978-1-5157-1124-7 (ebook PDF)

Editorial Credits
Jaclyn Jaycox, editor; Philippa Jenkins, designer;
Pam Mitsakos, media researcher; Steve Walker, production specialist

Photo Credits
Shutterstock: Birute Vijeikiene, 11, chromatos, 15, cynoclub, 3, backcover, davidkrug, 13, Gutzemberg, 1, 7,
Imageman, 19, red rose, design element used throughout, Roxana Bashyrova, cover, rsooll, 17, Sarah Fields
Photography, 5, small1, 9, Wutlufaipy, 21

Note to Parents and Teachers

The Cats, Cats, Cats set supports national science standards related to life
science. This book describes and illustrates short-haired cat breeds. The images
support early readers in understanding the text. The repetition of words and
phrases helps early readers learn new words. This book also introduces early
readers to subject-specific vocabulary words, which are defined in the Glossary
section. Early readers may need assistance to read some words and to use the
Table of Contents, Glossary, Read More, Internet Sites, Critical Thinking Using
the Common Core, and Index sections of the book.

Printed and bound in China
PO007732LEOF16

Table of Contents

Simple Hair Care

Cats are put into groups called breeds.
There are almost 100 cat breeds.
Some have short hair. Their coats
need very little care. Let's meet some
of these fun, friendly cats.

British Shorthair

The British Shorthair is known for its solid gray color. But it can be many colors and patterns. These cats are calm. But they usually don't like to be carried.

American Shorthair

The American Shorthair came to the United States on ships from England hundreds of years ago. The gray striped tabby is seen the most. These gentle cats make good pets.

Sphynx

The Sphynx is almost hairless.

Its body is covered with down.

A Sphynx's wrinkly skin can get

cold or sunburned easily.

Bombay

Bombays have flat, black fur and gold eyes. Bombays are smart pets. They can be trained to walk on leashes.

Siamese

Siamese cats are born with white coats. They soon grow dark areas called points on their faces, ears, paws, and tails. These blue-eyed cats meow a lot.

Abyssinian

Abyssinians look like small wildcats. Each hair has bands of two or more colors. This coat pattern is called ticked. These smart and friendly cats can learn to fetch.

Cornish Rex

The Cornish Rex has curly fur and whiskers. It has big eyes and tall ears on the top of its head. This playful pet is strong and fast.

Exotic

Exotics have soft, thick fur. They can be any color or pattern. These quiet cats like to snuggle. They are often called teddy bear cats.

Glossary

breed—a group of the same kind of animals

down—a soft covering of tiny hairs

fetch—to go get something and bring it back

pattern—a repeated shape or form

points—dark patches of fur on an animal's face, ears, paws, or tail

solid—one color

tabby—a cat with a striped and spotted coat

ticked—made of hair that has bands of two or more colors

Read More

Finne, Stephanie. *Exotic Shorthair Cats.* Checkerboard Animal Library. Minneapolis: ABDO Publishing, 2015.

Holland, Gini. *American Shorthairs.* Cats Are Cool. New York: PowerKids Press, 2014.

Olson, Gillia M. *Pet Cats Up Close.* Pets Up Close. North Mankato, Minn.: Capstone Press, 2015.

Internet Sites

FactHound offers a safe, fun way to find Internet sites related to this book. All of the sites on FactHound have been researched by our staff.

Here's all you do:

Visit *www.facthound.com*

Type in this code: 9781515709589

Check out projects, games and lots more at
www.capstonekids.com

Critical Thinking Using the Common Core

- The Abyssinian has a ticked coat pattern. What does ticked mean? (Craft and Structure)

- Choose two short-haired cats from this book. How are they alike? How are they different? (Key Ideas and Details)

- Which short-haired cat is your favorite? Why? (Integration of Knowledge and Ideas)

Index